Pure Adventure

Published by Outdoor Integrity Publishing Limited

22 Underley Hill,
Kendal, LA9 5EX
T: +44 (0)1539 723172

www.soaadventure.org

© Colin Mortlock, 2011.

All rights reserved. No part of the publication may be reproduced or transmitted in any form or by any means, electronic or mechanical, including photography, recording or any other information storage and retrieval system, without permission from Outdoor Integrity Publishing Limited.

The opinions expressed in this publication are those of the authors and do not necessarily represent those of the Editors or of Outdoor Integrity Publishing Limited.

ISBN 978-1-907362-01-9

British Library Cataloguing-in-Publication data

A catalogue record for this book is available from the British Library

Printed on stock from FSC accredited sources.

This monograph is taken from the opening keynote address at the fourth Outdoor Education Conference in Singapore 2010.

PURE ADVENTURE

Preliminary Remarks

Thank you for your invitation. The title of the conference, 'The Curious Garden', made me smile. I know from long experience that being curious, wanting to know what is around the corner, is **an instinct for adventure**. The word 'garden' also appealed. In old age I have, at last, come to love my garden flowers as I love wild flowers.

The title of my talk – Pure Adventure – is, as far as I know, a new term. It is based on universal values and ideals. I am convinced that properly implemented, this holistic concept could lead not only to a deep sense of individual wellbeing, but also make a major contribution to solving the problems facing the modern world. If Outdoor Education embraces this concept *in practice,* it will have come of age.

For 50 years I have sought to understand my relationship to wild Nature. For the last seven years I have become immersed in my subject. I live it in my head – trying to understand further, to find the simplest non-academic way of communicating what I have learnt and, more recently, how best to put these ideas into practice.

Let me share with you what happened in 2010.

In September 2009 *The Spirit of Adventure* was published, around 70 000 words and full of quotations to show that this was not just the views of one person. Then early in 2010 I received an invitation to visit Australia in June. I then worked for five months to reduce the 70 000 words to a basis for talks – around 18 000 words. From July I then worked for the next few months on further reducing the length to provide this talk for Singapore. It is now 8000 words, and hopefully clearer and more coherent.

The essence of my talk is this:

Wild nature, in its entirety (including the history of the human

race), is somehow embedded or encoded within the unconscious (or psyche) of each individual.

In other words, we are not just part of Nature, we *are* Nature. I make that statement with a considerable sense of awe and humility.

My faith in the capabilities of young people generally is *huge* – providing they are given the appropriate education and opportunities. I have seen mixed groups of 10–12 year olds undertake successful, self-reliant five-day expeditions over the Lake District hills and 100-mile kayak camping trips down the River Wye in Wales. These expeditions, under my responsibility, did not have the immediate presence of adults. That was 30 years ago. I would have hoped that by now, such expeditions would be commonplace, and even younger children involved. The opposite, of course, is the case.

Main Address

I would like to begin with a personal statement and to introduce five wisdoms.

I regard myself as no more and no less important than a blade of grass, a pebble or a tiny flower.

WISDOM ONE

You are shaped not only by your experiences but by your surroundings.

I know I have been shaped by two major forces:

- First by wild Nature rather than the man-made world (a very fortunate life outdoors, of both work and recreation).
- Second by Annette, my late wife and companion for nearly half a century. A truly remarkable lady, she was exceptionally gifted intellectually and highly accomplished in both arts and sciences. Her life was characterised by unselfish living – a truly inspirational person.

WISDOM TWO

Whatever life is about, it should include an unending search for truth.

A life dominated by fear and anxiety, or strong desires for money, status and power, will distract from that search.

WISDOM THREE

Quality action or quality experience must be balanced by quality reflection upon those actions or experiences.

A life of continuous action will never lead to any deep sense of wellbeing.

WISDOM FOUR

Learning is a lifelong process of which formal education is only a part. As long as you live you learn.

Learning can be divided into four areas: **Knowledge**, **Skills**, **Attitudes**, and **Concepts**.

- **Knowledge** – there has never been a time when knowledge is so easily obtained – literally at the press of a button. It is easily possible, however, to drown in a sea of knowledge. Knowledge and knowing are different. With experience comes a much deeper understanding, allowing a person to 'know'.

- **Skills** – are concerned with doing. There is no substitute for personal experience.

- **Attitude** – is always crucial. Is the glass half full or half empty? Ideally it should be the former – as expressed by the great virtue of vitality.

- **Concepts** – tend to be seen as big ideas that connect and give meaning to knowledge. Certainly this concept of 'Pure Adventure' is large.

WISDOM FIVE

Everything in Nature is dynamic.

The importance of this wisdom is immense. It means that the human being, a natural phenomenon, is not static – every aspect of a person is either:

progressing – growing or
regressing – going backwards, degenerating.

Now look at modern society in terms of this wisdom. Technology is obviously progressing – impressively so. But in terms of what is noble and worthwhile about being human, man is going backwards.

A quotation from a recent article in the international environmental magazine *Resurgence*:

'What we are only now beginning to register is the acute and profound social, spiritual, and psychological damage from half a century of unrestrained greed, a daily diet of advertising, over-consumption and a must-go-shopping mentality.'

Rampant consumerism is a more powerful global force than any previous religion.

In the comparatively short space of time man has been on the planet he has caused havoc, bringing destruction on the Earth itself, and on almost all life forms, including his own race.

In contrast to modern society's regression, wild Nature progresses, evolves and gets on with growing. Most people who experience wild Nature would agree that in contrast to the man-made world there is something very special about the natural world, perhaps something to do with concepts like **Freedom**, **Beauty** and **Truth**.

A Values Framework

In the introduction I said that the essence of my talk is that wild Nature, in its entirety, is embedded within the unconscious of each of us. In other words, beneath our separateness there is an underlying **unity**.

This section will look at a set of values that expresses that underlying unity. If these values are truly universal, then each of you should be broadly in agreement with them. They should feel as though they are 'along the right lines'.

Three questions are addressed:

- **Who am I?** }
- **Where am I going?** } And the 'I' refers to *any* human being.
- **How do I get there?** }

As a young person I was, of course, aware that external experiences affected me inwardly through my feelings. Yet outside me and inside me still seemed distinctly separate, because of the physical divide of my body. That feeling was dominant until I read a single sentence from *Markings*, the remarkable diary of Dag Hammarskjöld, one-time Secretary General of the United Nations. This is the sentence:

'The longest journey is the journey inwards.'

His use of the word 'journey', in a psychological context, was like finding a diamond. Instantly I realised the whole of my life, both inwards and outwards, was an amalgam of journeys. The outer experiences – the adventures with people and the environment, after careful reflection, were then funnelled into the mainstream inner journey – the longest adventure of them all. This inner journey was no less than the lifelong search for truth – for Who am I?, Where am I going? and How do I get there?

'Who Am I?'

The apparently simple question 'Who am I?' is profoundly complex. In my 70s I can confidently say, 'I am beginning to know myself'.

First an amazing fact – each of us is unique and so is every other animal, daisy, snowflake and leaf.

Second, from my reflections on personal experiences along with wide reading, I am sure that there is an underlying unity beneath our uniqueness.

- We are all natural.
- We all come from Nature and return to it.
- We are governed by natural forces. These are both external, e.g. weather, and internal, e.g. instincts.
- We all seek contentment.
- We all have the same aspects. These common aspects include:

A **physical** aspect – the body's importance in terms of deep wellbeing is immense.

A **mental** aspect – our intellect, home of our thinking. In a scientific and rational world, the danger is in over-emphasising its importance. It remains but one aspect. Bertrand Russell, the great Western philosopher, has a cogent quotation:

'Sell your cleverness and buy bewilderment' (or be-wild-er-ment).

An **emotional** aspect – our feelings, shallow and deep, positive and negative. A myriad of them, but two central ones – fear and love. For most of us, how we feel about something is ultimately more important than what we think about it.

A **spiritual** aspect – we all have something called 'spirit'. By far the most mysterious aspect, it is intangible. It does not appear to physically exist. Yet from the great writings of both East and West there is agreement about its supreme importance. If you deny this, then you deny the accumulated wisdom of the ages. Such denial is unfortunately commonplace, not least amongst those dominated by money, status and power.

I regard my spirit as my essence. I rejoice in the face that it never dies, and that everything in Nature has spirit, such as spirit of place. With regard to humans, I see spirit as having positive and negative aspects. The part relating to badness, evil and sin, the dark side, I regard as my shadow. That part concerned with the positive – the word goodness comes to mind – I regard as my **heart** or **conscience** or **soul**. These three words seem synonymous.

I love the simplicity of Cicero's words, **'The spirit is the true self.'**

I accept that **the spirit is the base of my values.** That statement could not be more important in terms of how I journey through my life because **all my actions depend on what I value.**

My values, my spirit and conscience, are based on my use of what are known as the **virtues** and **vices**.

I sense that all these traits lie in the unconscious, waiting to be activated. This leads me to another way of looking at who I am. I am both **conscious** and **unconscious**.

- **Conscious** self is everyday surface self: the self that meets all outer experiences.
- **Unconscious** self is the deeper sub-conscious self.

A good analogy perhaps is to imagine oneself as the ocean, in which the **surface** is the conscious self – which can range from flat calm to stormy – whilst **underneath the surface** lie immense depths – the unconscious. Between the conscious and the unconscious lies what has been termed –
'the enemy within', 'pseudo-self' or 'the false centre'.

This is **the ego**. It surrounds the conscious self, protects your uniqueness and emphasises your separateness. If you allow it to grow beyond self-respect, then it can quickly dominate. The ego incessantly demands gratification, but if you allow this, then you can become increasingly arrogant. Arrogance is the most ugly and divisive of vices. I was in my 40s when I happened to read, 'The size of a man's ego is in direct proportion to the length of the bonnet of his car'. As I had an E-type Jaguar at the time, I had nowhere to hide! Fortunately later experiences reduced my ego to a natural size. For those who lead very successful lives in a materialistic sense, there is a tendency for the ego to dominate.

Groups of people often display arrogance, or what might be termed group egotism, e.g. clubs, organisations, committees, families even. If they regard themselves as in any way superior or as an elite, then this is egotism. It is so common, it might well be described as a characteristic of modern living. The ego works against learning about the spirit and the unconscious.

'Where Am I Going?'

Once I have some idea of who I am, I need to try to establish where I am going, not just in my immediate living, but in terms of my whole life. Beneath consumer-driven, shallow and often false aims, e.g. a convenient and enjoyable lifestyle, fun and excitement, sex, shopping, being on TV, lie deeper aims. Throughout human history there has been a search for the meaning of human existence. This includes a search for truth – the meaning of beauty or freedom, and the nature of wisdom or happiness. I would suggest a simpler, more 'down to earth' answer to 'Where am I going?'.

I am going towards fulfilment, in all positive senses of being human. This means striving towards intellectual, physical, emotional, and spiritual maturity – this is or should be a lifelong process. Like the acorn, the seed of the oak, I aspire to become the giant oak tree.

Having looked at 'Who am I?' and 'Where am I going?', I now need to address the third question.

'How Do I Get There?'

The modern world is a complex and often dangerous place. In practice, a materialistic society tends to encourage the worship of money and power, status and selfishness. To live in this type of world, with a central aim of your positive growth in all senses, requires a strong personal **values framework**, which I also see as a universal values framework.

I see three components.

1. Act According to Conscience

Essentially this means trying to live by the virtues rather than their opposing vices (e.g. honesty not dishonesty, humility not arrogance).

It would seem common sense to regard the conscience as the battlefield between the good and the bad, between the virtues and the vices. It seems highly sensible to regard this battle as a lifelong process. With this approach, one can take heart from knowing one may well have the answer to the famous statement from William James, the American philosopher:

'The problem of man is to find a moral substitute for war.'

Your freedom is that, using your conscience, you choose between positive and negative aspects in all the billions of decisions you make over your lifetime.

The baseline virtue would appear to be **honesty**. To be ruthlessly honest, to be vigilant with one's self when reflecting on the experiences of one's life, is essential. It needs to become the strongest of habits. Growth, psychologically, comes through this struggle, as does a sense of wellbeing.

It may help to visualise your conscience as your moral or psychological spine. Like your spine, it needs to be upright and strong.

2. Try and Live By the Wisdoms

In use they are character strengths, expressing expertise in the conduct and meaning of life. They are akin to excellence. I have already mentioned five:

- Life as a search for truth

- Action balanced by reflection on the action
- All in Nature is dynamic
- Learning is a lifelong process
- We are shaped by our surroundings.

There are many more wisdoms to explore and be guided by. Here is just one new one at this stage:

We must develop an increasing sense of awe and wonder.

Without this wisdom it is not possible to take on the longest adventure, the inner journey, the search for the truth as to who you are. Refusal to embrace this wisdom is to indicate a fixation with self-importance. Egotism emphasises that a person is on the slippery slope of arrogance rather than on the path to humility.

3. Live with Maximum Awareness and Minimal Destruction of Nature

This third component is a combination of virtues and wisdoms. It is also holistic. The origin of this third parameter is as follows.

In 1997 I received an invitation to visit New Zealand to give one lecture at an international Outdoor Education conference, and I could say what I liked. But what to say? Sitting in my office with a blank sheet of A4, within minutes I wrote down the following:

'Everything in Nature is alive in its own way – is on its own adventurous journey and deserves its own wellbeing. Everything in Nature, from a grain of sand to a star, from the tiniest flower to a human being, is of no more and no less importance than anything else.'

Those words had arisen from my unconscious into my conscious. I sense strongly that I had been shaped by my wild surroundings during those years of solo expeditions, and wild Nature was using me as a conduit to express herself to the materialistic human world.

Now, 12 years later, I am convinced that this 'wilderness statement' should be the basis of civilisation itself. It creates a level playing field, not just for all humans, but, using common sense, for everything in Nature.

An Elemental Trinity

For ten years, after an early retirement from an increasingly bureaucratic and materialistic world of education, life had seemed good. It was a life of long solo expeditions in big mountains and along wilderness coastlines. Annette, when not teaching, would join me. Then I was hit as if by a sledgehammer. This very fit lady with three tough, month-long expeditions in 2002, was dead from cancer by May the following year. For the next five years I sought to understand the significance of her life and how her values related to my own. Eventually there came genuine glimmerings of understanding. These focus on three words, which I term an elemental trinity:
unity – love – adventure.

The first word is **Unity**.

Here are three key incidents from my life – all with the same message.

- In 1981 I was attempting the first night crossing by kayak from the Lake District to the Isle of Man – a 40 mile open crossing. After an inspiring 10 miles paddling into a glorious sunset, it had become very dark. I could still see, but my mood had become gloomy. There was a huge bank of sea mist to the south, and no sight of land in any direction. Being alone I felt the exposure acutely. Suddenly I was aware of a tiny bird fluttering around the kayak, more like a large butterfly than a bird, and I realised this was my first sighting of a storm petrel, the tiniest of seabirds, weighing around 28 grams. After a minute or so it had gone. I mused at such a meeting – it was almost as though the bird was as curious about me as I was excited about it. I carried on west into the darkness, but there was now one huge difference. My pessimism and gloom had been replaced by optimism and warm feelings. Years later I realised the significance of this meeting. My separateness, my loneliness, had been suspended. I had felt a unity with the storm petrel.

- In 1979 I had undertaken a 1200km sea-kayak expedition up the coast of Alaska with a friend. Two years later I returned for a 1000km solo trip. During the first week, when on the water, I became increasingly aware of something very unusual happening to me psychologically. While my awareness of my surroundings was as acute as possible (because of the many dangers), I also found myself going ever deeper into my unconscious. This inner awareness remained with me for the rest of the expedition when on the water.

On return to England, I found I had a very strong urge to try and understand what had happened. I found I had become a pilgrim as well as an adventurer. Years later I began to understand. At its simplest, somehow the ocean had to be encoded or imprinted within me, in my unconscious. Then that part of my unconscious had become conscious. It was as if a button within me, marked ocean, had been pressed. This oceanic experience was an example of a concept named by Carl Jung as the **collective unconscious**. This was the idea that the whole of wild Nature was imprinted within us.

A few years later the validity of this concept was confirmed. If I may continue with the button analogy, this time the button that had been pressed within me was marked 'wild flowers'.

- A summer morning – I had gone to check out a new scramble in a rarely visited ravine in the Lake District. At the foot of the climb was a solitary tall plant with striking dark-blue flowers. My whole attitude to flowers up to that moment was one of disinterest – they were something for the ladies and certainly not of interest to me, a serious adventurer. I completed the climb. Almost unbelievably, at the top there was one more flower – of the same type! I knew then I had to find out what it was, though I had never had such a desire previously. Annette, a keen botanist, gave me the answer – *Aquilegia vulgaris*, also known as the eagle flower.

It was the beginning of a love affair with flowers which still exists today. For a couple of years it became my number one passion – trying to find different wild flowers and the challenge of identification. I was later to realise this new adventure was of huge significance in my maturation – it took me out of my self-centredness. I was now into the exciting and very beautiful world of flowers. My ego was vanishing quickly – how could I tell my friends that my next adventure was a hunt for flowers!

Those three experiences – the storm petrel, Alaska and the flower in the Lakes – along with another six or so other unusual incidents, left me in no doubt that they had the same message. I wrote this in 2002:

'I know that deep down I have a unity with Nature because I have experienced that unity.'

This wisdom has been around for a very long time. For example:

Chuang-Tzu, 4BC:
'I and all things in the universe are one.'

Meister Eckhart, 1260-1328:
'All that man has eternally here in multiplicity is intrinsically one... this is the deepest depth.'

And more recently, in 1983, David Bohm, physicist, wrote:
'Every part of the universe contains the whole universe enfolded within it.'

In the 1980s, Norway witnessed its biggest ever environmental protest, in the far north. The government proposed to build a hydro-electric dam on a main river to provide electricity from which the locals would benefit. The local Laplanders fiercely objected. When asked why, their reply was classic:

'Never, the river here is part of us.'

Many of you will be familiar with some aspects of this fascinating area. Jung's **moments of synchronicity**, Maslow's **peak experiences**, Csikzentmihalyi and his concept of **flow**, and the phrase from modern sport of **'in the zone'**.

I have a bulging file of accounts of other people's unusual or what are often termed 'transcendental' experiences. They have common elements:

- Almost always unexpected
- Occur when alone, or feel alone
- Occur at any age (the youngest example I have is aged seven)
- Occur anywhere, although wild Nature and churches are frequent locations.

All, I believe, have the same underlying message:

In the moment(s) of the experience your separateness is suspended.

Put simply, you have feelings of unity.

I am convinced that these 'out of the ordinary experiences' are common and that they happen to most people. I would be surprised, for example, if the majority of you cannot recollect such moments. Moments like these are remembered with startling clarity, even if they happened many years before.

If you in any way doubt the importance of unity, then consider this fact. No human being would be here on the planet if it were not for the unity of two people. I refer here not simply to a physical union, but hopefully the unity of feelings of love.

What disturbs and saddens me is that I feel this knowledge has been either deliberately side-lined or conveniently ignored. As far as I am aware such 'unity' is not a part of education, nor outdoor education, nor discussions on adventure, and certainly not a popular topic of conversation. I am convinced that awareness of these experiences and their meaning have a major positive message in a troubled, divisive modern world.

The second key word of the trilogy is **Love**.

Devastated after Annette's death in 2003, I moved from the Lakes to live remotely in Scotland. Deeply depressed, I was also very puzzled: in the final weeks of her life, Annette kept insisting she was in a 'bubble of happiness'.

I was determined to try to understand, not only what that phrase meant, but also what her values were, and how they compared with my own. Was there a bridge between them? We were very different people.

My **values** at that time centred around **ten virtues.** As I wandered the unfrequented hills, seeing little of their beauty, inevitably I set these virtues against how Annette had lived the detail of her life. Again and again I went through it. She seemed to possess all ten. This seemed wrong – my experience was that people were like myself, a mixture of virtues and vices. I thought I must be biased – putting her on a pedestal.

I checked with her friends. Only one vice appeared. One person thought she talked too much! Knowing the person concerned, I was doubtful. More likely this trait was largely positive – the great virtue of **vitality** perhaps, and a reflection of her enthusiasm for life. Finally I rang the headmistress at her school. After chiding me for being so depressed – 'did I not realise how very lucky I had been to be her partner?' – she made a simple comment:

'Everyone, both pupils and staff in both primary and secondary schools, loved Annette.'

That comment, the focus on that word **love** was fascinating. I knew that she loved her fellow humans – of all ages and all types – even smiling and talking to individuals she knew had irritated or angered me.

I also knew, especially from our expeditions together, her delight at being in Nature, whether in her garden or on an expedition, that she loved Nature in its entirety. Her expedition diaries, complete with paintings, were full of sketches of Nature, from landscape and flora, to slugs and marmots.

I found reading about love extremely valuable. The great writings from both East and West, over thousands of years, were in strong accord:

Love, in its universal sense, is simply the most important word in any language.

Having discovered Annette's values centred on love, I still had to relate them to my own. I decided to write to myself, as writing can often help clarify a jumbled mind. I finished up with about 50 sheets of A4, ending in a morass of 25 virtues and opposing vices. I remained confused, until someone suggested I had a look at *St Paul's Letter to the Corinthians*. I had missed the obvious.

St Paul's letter describes nine components of love. Eight of them were in my original list of 10 virtues.

You might ask at this point, 'But what about the other 17 virtues you discovered?' The answer could not be simpler. Those remaining 17, and indeed all virtues, are aspects of universal love. I find it easiest to visualise the connection in this way:

Love is the circle. Each virtue is a segment of this circle. You are the circle.

Once I had discovered that love was the most important word, I realised I had seldom used the word in my writings and lectures. Even in my personal life I had seen it as something separate – restricted to the remarkable feelings of romantic love. Then I remembered why I had left my kayak in Alaska after the first expedition. Overwhelmed by Alaska's magnificence I had actually stated that '*I loved Alaska*'. That memory triggered another from that expedition – literally an unforgettable moment. This occurred on the last full day – a 12-hour epic that placed considerable physical and psychological demands on me. By evening I was on the outer coast, a lee shore, and in a rising gale. It was raining, becoming dark, and I was surrounded by waves exploding on reefs. Staying upright was becoming increasingly difficult. Suddenly there came a flash of insight: it did not matter if I died.

Years previously I had come across an Old Norse saying:

'The most important thing in life is to die at the right time'.

For me this meant, 'We all die sometime. Try to make sure that when you go, it is when you are doing something you love.' I loved sea canoeing and I loved Alaska.

This reflection on love led me to a possible reason why Annette, in her final weeks, had insisted she was in a 'bubble of happiness'. In the '*Oxford Book of Death*' I had come across the following:

'How you face death depends on how you lived your life.'

I knew from nearly half a century with her, that she had lived her life, almost whatever her surroundings, with unselfish love. Here was something we shared. We had both faced death with equanimity – because we loved what we were doing, even if my love was narrowly focussed in comparison to her universal love.

Subsequent to Alaska, and especially after 1992 when I retired, I realised eventually that I too loved wild Nature in its entirety and was never happier than when on an expedition.

There was another extremely valuable message concerning love from Annette's life. This was her **vitality**. There is a wisdom that the best type of lifestyle, the most rewarding, is that which is essentially unselfish, and where you love each moment of your existence, or what is popularly described as 'living in the now'.

I realised, with some awe and wonder, that what had taken me most of my life to understand, she had practised throughout her life in the most natural and spontaneous of manners. The matron in the hospice confided in me her sense of awe at Annette's life in her final weeks – largely spent comforting others who found death so very difficult to face. Annette's best friend, herself a victim of breast cancer, echoed a similar confidence. She stated that, if it had been possible, she would have died that Annette might live.

This has left me in no doubt whatsoever of the importance of another wisdom:

The quality of a person should be seen by how they live the detail of their life.

This is much more important than their specific achievements.

In President Obama's inauguration speech there is mention of no less than 20 virtues. Professor Elizabeth Alexander of Yale University composed the poem to end that speech. It contains the following:

'What if THE word is LOVE, love beyond marital, filial, national? Love that casts a widening pool of light.'

The final word of my trilogy – after unity and love, is **Adventure**.

In the 1920s Professor Whitehead of Harvard and Cambridge Universities made his famous comment:

'Without adventure civilisation is in full decay.'

Towards 100 years on from when he made this remark, I would stress that civilisation now is in very severe decay, despite all our technological achievements. I would humbly suggest a single-word addition to his quotation so that it becomes:

'Without *pure* adventure civilisation is in full decay'

Let me explain. I see adventure in two senses. The first is the conventional narrow one, relating to specific adventure activities – mountaineering, surfing, kayaking, sailing and so on. The second is what might be termed adventure in the broad major sense. This is where you accept positively that the whole of your life ahead will always be a journey of uncertainty. In other words you accept that this longest journey will also be the longest adventure. You suspect it may also be the most challenging adventure of them all, as it affects the entire detail of how you live the rest of your life.

Essentially this means accepting your unconscious as well as your conscious. You reject the modern emphasis of living almost exclusively at a fast pace

on the surface of yourself, in the land of separateness. Instead you seek wellbeing through trying to find those elusive feelings of unity by reflecting on your actions or experiences – unity within yourself, unity with others, unity with the natural environment.

An anecdote may help here.

In August 1968 Bernard Moitessier set sail in the first round-the-world single-handed yacht race. Seven months later he had rounded the three great capes of Good Hope, Leuwin and the Horn. The hardest section was now behind him. He had crossed his outward track and he was leading the race by a considerable distance. He needed to turn north and head up the Atlantic back to Plymouth. He did no such thing. He carried on eastwards eventually to finish up with friends in Tahiti. If he had headed north and if there had been a huge signpost it would have said: 'To success and egoland'. If there had been another giant signpost pointing in the direction he did take, it would very likely have had the following words: 'Towards understanding, wellbeing and fulfilment'.

The press of the day were totally bemused by his actions. For no apparent reason he had rejected an outstanding chance of winning the race – a race that had attracted worldwide interest, and would have guaranteed his fame, as well as making him rich. In a materialistic world dominated by the importance of success, and the ensuing trappings of wealth, status and power, he was ridiculed. In reality he had chosen a Pure Adventure approach to his sailing. He knew that the activity he loved would only bring a deep sense of wellbeing if he rejected the shallow and self-centred aims of materialism.

The temptations for the individual to succumb to adulation, which is so adored by the media and its audiences, are huge. Yet such temptations need to be fiercely resisted, and not least by those who are famous adventurers.

Returning now to personal experiences and subsequent reflection. In 1984 I wrote *The Adventure Alternative*, a young man expressing his enthusiasm for adventure for all young people. I gradually realised there was a downside to conventional adventure. By definition it was not only exciting being 'on the edge', but inevitably egocentric or at least self-centred. Not only that, adrenalin was a drug. It was all too easy to become addicted. The phrase 'adrenalin junkies' has been commonly applied to those who have to go into wild Nature for their fix. Those are strong critical remarks, because I was one of them – from a devotion to rock climbing, then on to white-water kayaking, then to open-boat catamaran sailing and so on.

Then, and thank goodness, my adventure turned increasingly solo – where competition became meaningless and egotism both stupid and shallow.

The period later in my life when I fell in love with wild flowers was especially significant, because that passion was both outside myself and not dependent on adrenalin. It also led, eventually, to my becoming aware that I related to wild Nature in her entirety.

I have coined the phrase 'Pure Adventure' because the great virtue of purity comes to mind when I see the unpolluted wonders of wild Nature – from the tiniest flower to a majestic mountain – and because

I know that purity is embedded in my unconscious. Impurity, in contrast, obviously comes from the use of the vices so characteristic of the man-made world. The huge temptation to succumb to the desires of money, status and power can very quickly destroy our original, more natural being.

You may be tempted to ask, 'How important is this stuff about Pure Adventure?', especially as narrow adrenalin adventure demands many key virtues – such as determination, self-reliance and co-operation. My response would be 'it could not be more important'.

Allow me to revisit my concern for the direction of the modern world. Currently the human race faces formidable problems. These include:

- Global warming and increasingly extreme and unpredictable weather
- Pollution – of our air, soil and water
- Economic and financial extremism
- Over-population
- Trivialisation (dumbing down)
- An accelerating and increasingly fragmented man-made world
- Obesity
- Drugs
- Power, in practice, driven by individuals without integrity and characterised by arrogance, greed and other vices.

In the 1920s Professor Whitehead said that **any** civilised society will display five characteristics:

- Adventure
- Truth
- Beauty
- Peace
- Art.

My contention is that their opposites tend to be characteristic of the

modern world:
- Timidity not adventure
- Dishonesty not truth
- Conflict not peace
- Ugliness not beauty
- Art - a subjective matter, of course, but I suspect ugly or meaningless art is more commonplace today.

We need to work towards creating a civilised world that does exhibit these five positive characteristics. Unless we are successful in this challenge, then I believe the human race may well have no future in any civilised sense. Despite all the good work going on around the world, in reality this is minimal in comparison to all the on-going destruction of the planet and its life forms.

The radical problems facing us demand radical solutions. Here is one. We need (and by 'we' I refer especially to young people, the citizens of tomorrow) to revisit wild Nature as our true home.

Thoreau, like many before him, expressed this wisdom in a famous statement:

'In wilderness lies the preservation of the world.'

This solution, however, will only work if we go into the 'university of the wilderness' with some understanding of how we relate to it. We need to journey as pilgrims as well as adventurers.

For a start we could take Whitehead's five characteristics with us when we immerse ourselves in the outdoors. They are characteristic of wild Nature and we need to be as aware of them as possible.

I will comment on each of the five:

- **Art**
  I see art as demonstrating the spiritual and the sacred. The canvas of Nature leaves me with a sense of awe and wonder at the artist who created such magnificence.

- **Beauty**
  Is everywhere in wild Nature. The more the awareness, both macro and micro, the more beauty there is to see.

- **Peace**
  Peace and quiet are characteristic of so much of wild Nature – feelings of timelessness are commonplace; eternal rhythms in contrast to the frenetic pace and noise of the modern world.

- **Truth**
  When I adventured on the rock face and mountain, the river and the ocean, when I was on the edge of my capabilities, I was facing the truth of the matter, the natural examination I had set myself. In other words, 'Was I up to the challenge?'.

- **Adventure**
  As a major characteristic of any civilised society, as I have explained, this needs to be changed to *Pure* Adventure. If it remains narrow adventure then the emphasis is on going into wild Nature and taking from it exciting and worthwhile activities that tend to be specialist and self-centred in an egotistic sense. Pure Adventure accepts that everything in Nature is on its own adventure and deserves its own wellbeing. This approach also accepts the underlying unity of everything in Nature.

Modern societies are built on fear – driven by making money and seeking security. Pure Adventure is built on love and unity, not fear and materialism.

Final Reflections

Progressing from my early climbing days, when I treated wild Nature as an open-air sports hall for rock gymnastics, to realising that I was part of Nature, was a large step in my understanding. To then move on to realising, knowing in my depths, that **I am Nature** was a giant step. Unsurprisingly my attitude to life has been radically affected, and not least how I view outdoor learning.

A memory surfaces of sometime around 1990, when I visited a famous PE college to assess their advanced qualification in Outdoor Education. I was met at the gate by a deputation of the students headed by an adviser in Outdoor Education, whose words shook me. They were to the effect that they were near the end of their course and yet they still did not know what Outdoor Education meant! It did not take long to discover the cause of the problem. Like most courses of this type, there was a mixture of environmental, academic and adventure activity modules – most of which were taught to a high standard. What was missing was a 'values framework' that linked all the modules.

Now, 20 or so years later, I can see that example of 'a course in bits', even if the bits are first class, is but a reflection of what may well be **the major problem** that lies at the heart of the modern world.

This is well-expressed by this quotation from David Bohm, writing in the 1980s:

'Throughout history fragmentation has produced severe and destructive conflict on every level. This fragmentation ultimately may threaten the very existence of humanity.'

Another word for fragmentation is specialisation. We live in an age of specialisation, if not extreme specialisation.

Duane Elgin, an American also writing in the 1980s, in his book *Beyond Ego,* puts his finger on the problem with this single sentence:

'We are engaged in a race between self-destruction and self-discovery.'

Thirty years on from when that comment was made, I sense we now urgently need to win that race. To bring his sentence into 2010 I would lengthen it as follows

'We are engaged in a race between self-destruction and the self-discovery that beneath our uniqueness there is an underlying

unity with Nature.'

That underlying 'unity with Nature', or 'the way of the Tao', became a wonderful reality for me personally during those 10 years of mainly long solo expeditions after I retired from education.

I found a deep sense of wellbeing in a lifestyle based on the eternal rhythms of Nature rather than the complex demands of modern living. The elements that made these journeys so attractive were twofold. First they were basic:

- A very simple lifestyle – trek from dawn to dusk/eat/camp/sleep
- Always over new ground (the uncertainty that is adventure)
- Surroundings of beauty
- Surroundings of friends even when 'alone'
- An element of natural, rather than man-made, danger
- The purity, naturalness and honesty of the wilderness.

Secondly the whole of my being – mentally, physically, emotionally and spiritually – tended to be involved in the most natural way. It was certainly one of the happiest and most satisfying periods of my life.

In the last few years I have begun to see why this feeling of unity with everything in Nature is supremely important.

In my introductory remarks I said that the essence of my talk was that wild Nature in its entirety was in some way imprinted or embedded in the unconscious of each individual. This included the entire history of the human race. That history, despite all the magnificent achievements, is very seriously marred by a stain of evil acts – unacceptable behaviour, epitomised by the seven deadly sins. The debate over whether man is naturally good or bad has continued throughout history. My contention is that man is naturally good, but has allowed himself to succumb to the seductive temptations of the man-made world. Not only that, but the concept of man being superior to everything else in Nature is not only wrong, but will eventually destroy the human species – the evidence is all around us.

Mencius, the Chinese philosopher, points the way we need to go:

'The tendency of man's nature to be good is like the tendency of water to flow downhill.'

What he is saying in effect is that, apart from modern man, Nature gets on with the process of growing naturally and progressing – which is all positive and good news. The critical point is this – the whole history of mankind, both good and bad, is a *tiny percentage* of the whole of wild Nature. In other words, as wild Nature is imprinted in each of us, then *our* basic Nature is massive good news, indeed startlingly good news.

As I write this, from my memory comes the image of a high mountain bivouac on an open ridge looking east, and the arrival of dawn very slowly over what seemed an endless vista of mountain ranges and valleys. I felt awe and wonder at the beauty. The eternal words from the *Upanishads* came to mind as I watched:

'What is without us is within us, and what is within us is without us.'

I know in my depths that wild Nature is imprinted within. This means, potentially, that there can be no more important area of learning than Outdoor Education. It must be seen, however, as holistic – as expressed by the concept of Pure Adventure and not as unrelated 'bits', regardless of the quality of the latter.

In other words, whatever aspect of Nature you are concerned with – from high adventure to environmental activities, from conservation to creative arts – your attitude needs to be holistic. It should also be humble and never arrogant. The corruption that is so endemic in the man-made world will not only remain but accelerate if egotism remains dominant. Man needs to be highly aware of his natural roots, wherein lies the deeper and more remarkable self.

If you look at the website for the Spirit of Adventure Foundation – set up as a charity to promote the values I have outlined in this talk – and my latest book, you will see amongst the ideals:

All young people who live in the modern world to undertake self-reliant expeditions relevant to their needs and abilities and eventually without adults. They need to undertake those journeys aware of the Pure Adventure concept.

I used to believe energy was the driving force behind all of Nature. I now prefer the term **positive energy**, which is **love**.

I believe **love** is synonymous with the following words, in their deepest or purest of senses:

- With peace
- With freedom
- With beauty
- With wisdom
- With goodness
- With unity
- With adventure.

Some climbers have reported that during an epic fall off the rock face, their whole life has flashed in front of them before they hit the ground. Something slightly similar happened to me during my intense depression immediately after Annette's death. Her 50 years or so with me flashed in detail before my eyes. I knew with certainty that if those who have the power in this world could live the detail of their lives as she had lived hers, then we would not have the problems we face today.

If your heart is in the same place as mine, then please embrace these ideas – and make a reality of Pure Adventure.

Thank you for your time.

(The address was given to an audience of 600+ and was very well received.)